A GIFT FOR YOU

To express my appreciation for your purchase of this exquisite lifestyle cookbook, I am delighted to extend an exclusive gift to you.

Receive a complimentary coaching session with Elle Jolie Wellness as my way of saying thank you.

Scan the QR code to start your wellness journey today!

LOVE | AMBIANCE | FOOD

BISTRO BENE!

A beautiful love, ambiance and food book that will inspire your daily entertaining experiences in a way your family and friends will never forget... Grab your latte and I'll meet you inside where the magic lies.

ELLE JOLIE

To my beautiful and ridiculously strong wildlings. Who are always hell-bent on squeezing the lovely marrow out of each life event. Without you, this book would not exist.

– Love, Mumma

Table of Contents

Summer...5

Autumn...59

Winter...107

Spring...129

*LOVE

...is the ability to put affection into every bite. Some say it's a gift. I say it's an honour to show the people in your life that there is no other place you would rather be than providing sustenance in a beautiful kitchen that resonates with music, delicious fragrances, and ultimate joy! As your pots and pans create the energy of nurture, you will find yourself in a constant state of friendship, filled with variance in age and companionship. Your heart will forget what a lonely beat is, and the world in which you live will be forever satisfied.

FOOD

By listening to the different palatable needs of each of my guests as I served recipes from this collection, my menu evolved to a place of good choice and nutrition with seemingly little effort. When you spend the time creating a kitchen that is high functioning, you will be able to focus your energy on the replenishment of goods and on skill development, rather than chaotic disorganization. Playing with your recipe choices in a relaxed mindset will soothe and nourish all those around you, taking the stress off of the end result and teaching you how to live in the "food moment".

SUMMER

"Oh the place I long to linger"

Camping Magic...

The Rockwood-Roo...

When my conscious intention of living with more colour and texture was realized, who knew that a simple trailer like the **"Rockwood-Roo"** would become the biggest surprise on four wheels. I sit in the space of delight and wonder, smelling the purple of the borscht on the stove. I embrace the resonance of Bon Iver as I look out over the watery eye-candy of my **Woodlake Paradise**. It is here that I desire to share with you...

CREATING SPACES...

Oh I beg you to reconsider your camping-ness. Lets move from **"calamity"** to **"crazy fantastic"**. Camping life is special... layer it like it is. Organization and a firm foundation in your home should lend an openness to how you think of your trailer. The space you inhabit for your holiday should evoke a feeling of pure **delight**, created by you for the people you love the most.

To reform your trailer into such a state of **delight**, you need an organized plan that goes something like this:
- decide on a **three-colour** plan that excites you
- a trip to Benjamin Moore to buy three gallons of a high-adhesive product called "Styx", your very best friend
- sanding supplies
- all your paint drop-cloths
- a short-cut brush (I no longer tape for paint projects)
- three weeks of three-hour blocks per day, completely focused
- rip out all hideous fabric out and replace with **fresh-eyed** choices... new draperies as well
- sand all cupboard material, paint three coats of "Styx" and two coats of finishing colour
- layer and decorate to your **heart's** content

PEELING BACK THE LAYERS...

In any environment, the foundation is key. **Super-succinct** organization, great colour, creative flooring, and learning to disguise eye-sores allows your energy to feel at ease, creating positive, **solution-based** thoughts. For example, turning the useless couch into a daybed allows for more **lounging** room and a permanent sleep space for a little person. If you look closely, I use attractive blankets to hide large, ugly openings under the master bed, which are also a storage space for clothing.

FEAR has no place in your design life - be **bold**, **brazen**, and open to **"mucker-uppers"**. Screwing something up is an opportunity to step back and reassess calmly. Something **Kismet** might happen in your little disaster and turn it into a **Pandora's Box** of good fortune. You may even find yourself **smiling** while learning to create environmental **balance**.

This bit of **creamsicle** heaven has created quite a stir on the gorgeous waters of Wood Lake, where **turtles** float about on the little pond outside my door, while hours are spent on the dock creating **friendships** faster than butterflies flutter. An awakening of sorts is this place of **serendipitous** fun and frolic.

Being mocked a little for my camping **"fairy magic"** seems just about right as my latte friends show up at my door. Submitting to the zone of true **family** time, where the internet is a stranger but you can see the **smiles** on your children's faces as they catch their first and tenth fish, it **settles** your mind into a place of home where the air finds you **breathing** well.

TASTES LIKE MORE

I awaken in this summer oasis as we allow ourselves to **"puddle"** in the heat of the day. Then in the evening, when our stomachs rumble, we find refuge in the mini **gourmet** space, where the celebration of all our elements meets the **exuberance** of what we have once again created in humble luxury.

GRAINY MASHED POTATOES

1/2 c. of butter
2 tbsp. grainy dijon mustard
1/2 c. of half & half cream
kosher salt & fresh ground pepper, to taste

- in medium sized pot, boil potatoes until tender, drain
- add butter, mustard, cream, salt and pepper
- whip potatoes, with hand mixer, until light and fluffy

BORSCHT

12 c. chicken or beef broth
2 big cans of diced tomatoes
4 bay leaves (remove before serving)
1 lg. white onion, diced
3 c. beets, cleaned and cut into bite-sized chunks
2 c. baby potatoes
2 handfuls of fresh dill
kosher salt & fresh ground pepper

- put all ingredients into a large pot
- bring to a boil until beets are tender
- simmer for 30min.
- serve with a dollop of sour cream and fresh dill
- season with salt & pepper
- *ya you did...muah!!!*

SUGGESTED SERVING:

- serve on a bed of grainy mashed potatoes with a mild Italian sausage

BEERGARITA

1 can limeade
4 beer
1 c. tequila
white goose berries

- stir gently
- serve over ice
- feel free to add a sugar/ salt rim to your glass
- *danger alert!*

Warmed Potato Salad

make 30min. before serving

1 lb. fingerling potatoes
1/2 lb. bacon (approx. 12 strips) ~ Harvest Bacon is the "bomb piggity"

Dressing

1/2 c. sour cream
1/2 c. mayonnaise
1/4 c. lemon juice
handful fresh dill
handful scallions or chives

- boil potatoes until firmly tender, drain, set aside
- using a deep frying pan, fry bacon until desired consistency. I like ours moderately crunchy
- keep fat and bacon in the pan
- mix together well
- add dressing to the bacon pieces & fat
- add potatoes
- toss & toss
- serve
- *watch grown men eat it out of the bowl, while little men pick out all of the bacon…delight!*

WATERMELON BASIL SALAD

1 md. watermelon, cut into bite-sized chunks
12 fresh basil leaves, torn nicely
1 sm. red onion, diced
fresh blackberries (optional)

DRESSING

1/4 c. canola oil or avocado oil
1/4 c. Mirabello balsamic vinegar
kosher salt & fresh ground pepper, to taste

- whisk and add to watermelon
- *put on a shmexy platter*

"O HONEY DEW, MEET YOUR FENNEL FRIEND" SALAD

1 honeydew melon, cut into bite-sized chunks
1 fennel bulb, cored, thinly sliced
segments of 1 orange (optional)
2 shallots, thinly sliced
2 tbsp. apple cider vinegar
juice of 2 oranges
1/2 c. canola oil
basil (optional)

- *dress beautifully with edible accessories ~ such a fresh palate-cleansing delight!*

Once upon a time there was a mango. She was lonely for beef so they dated... in this salad

3 mangos, chopped
3 cucumbers, chopped
2 handfuls cilantro, chopped
3 pickled jalapenos, chopped, seeds removed
3 tbsp. lime juice
3 tbsp. canola oil
splash jalapeno juice

- add beef filet
- *mix it up, people...mix it up!*

Beef Fillet

* needs marinating

beef fillet, approx. 5" thick
3 oz. espresso
3 tbsp. Mirabello balsamic vinegar
2 tbsp. minced garlic
kosher salt & fresh ground pepper, to taste

- marinate in ingredients above for at least 1 hour
- season generously with salt & pepper
- pan sear till crisp & finish in oven at 425°F for 5-15 mins
- *...nothing like a good piece of meat*

Serving Suggestion:

- use for mango salad and beef sliders

BEEF SLIDERS

slider buns
thin slices of beef filet
"wasabi mayo"

WASABI MAYO

1/2 c. mayonnaise
3 tbsp. wasabi (I use Inglehoffer wasabi horseradish)
2 tbsp. minced garlic
2 scallions

- mix and apply to beef sliders/buns
- *yummyyy*

"RED DEER" SAUCE

1/2 c. rice vinegar
1/4 c. sesame oil
2 tbsp. garlic (or a little more if you like)
2 tbsp. ginger
1 tbsp. soy sauce
kosher salt & fresh ground pepper

- mix & drizzle majority of the sauce while grilling, keeping some aside for dipping

PRAWNS, 10 OR SO

10 Prawns (or so)

- *I spend the bucks on these at the fish market for an extravagant summer meal… they are worth it!*

DIGGIN' IN

BUTTERMILK CAKE

1 1/2 c. butter, softened
2 1/4 c. white sugar
3 eggs separated/divorced
1 1/2 tsp. Grand Marnier
3 1/2 c. flour
1 tbsp. baking powder
1 tsp. baking soda
2 1/4 c. buttermilk

- in a stand-up mixer, beat butter with 2 c. sugar until fluffy
- beat in egg yolks, one at a time
- beat in Grand Marnier
- in a separate bowl, whisk together flour, baking powder, and baking soda. Mix into butter mixture alternately with buttermilk
- in another bowl, beat egg whites with remaining 1/4 c. sugar until soft peaks form
- fold one quarter at a time into batter until all used up
- scrape into lined parchment pans (grease then add paper)
- bake at 350°F for 50min. or until skewer comes out clean
- *dreamy masterpiece*

BLUEBERRY COMPOTE

use any combo of fruit and use as a fresh jam which stores for weeks

4 c. blueberries
lg. splash of Grand Marnier
1 c. white sugar

- simmer 30min. or until mixture is a thick consistency

WHIPPED CREAM TOPPING

2 c. whipping cream
1/4 c. sugar
1 tbsp. Grand Marnier

- whip cream, sugar, and Grand Marnier together
- with a friend, layer cake, compote, and cream
- sprinkle with "Nerds" candy
- *eat it!!!*

More Culinary Camping Magic

Maple Dressing

1/3 c. canola oil
1 tbsp. pomegranate balsamic vinegar or red wine
2 tbsp. maple syrup
1 tsp. dijon mustard
kosher salt & fresh ground pepper, to taste

The Aussie Salad

2 c. raspberries
2 c. cherry tomatoes
1/2 c. goat cheese, crumbled
2 oranges, cut into slices
seeds from 2 pomegranates
1/2 red onion, diced
8-10 cooked beets

- *inspired by the cute boat boy on Turtle Bay*

Beets

8-10 md. beets, cleaned and cut
1/4 c. oil
juice of 2 oranges
kosher salt & fresh ground pepper, to taste

- cook beets in oil, orange juice, and salt & pepper
- bake at 425°F until tender
- set aside to cool
- layer with rest of salad ingredients
- drizzle with maple dressing
- *make it gorgeous!*

Poison Ribs

Boiling Mixture

4 gallons water
1 c. soy sauce
1/3 c. anise seed
8 green onions
1/2 c. fresh grated ginger
freshly grated lemon rind

Marinade

1 c. hoisin sauce
1/2 c. sugar
juice of 1 lemon
1 tbsp. soy sauce
2 tbsp. rice vinegar
fresh ginger
sesame seeds, for garnish

- boil ribs in boiling mixture for 1hr.
- cut into rib sized pieces
- drain, rinse, & place on baking sheet
- slather on marinade and broil until crispy
- keep your eye on it!
- serve with "Crunchy Rice" or "Smashed Tatoes"
- *anyone who eats them is under your spell*

Smashed Tatoes

5 lg. russet potatoes, cut into bite-sized chunks
  ~ keep the skins on!
6 c. water
1/4 c. butter
1/4 c. heavy cream
kosher salt & fresh ground pepper, to taste

- boil potatoes until tender
- drain
- smash with a masher
- add butter, cream, salt and pepper
- *call it a day!*

Crunchy Rice

3-4 c. rice
1/3 c. virgin coconut oil
kosher salt & fresh ground pepper, to taste

- cook up your favorite rice according to instructions
- in a deep skillet, heat coconut oil
- add rice, salt & pepper and saute until super crunchy, approx. 20-25min.

"WHEN LAMB HANGS WITH BEEF... THIS HAPPENS" BURGERS

1/2 lb. ground beef
1/2 lb. ground lamb
1 egg
1/2 c. panko
2 tbsp. Mirabello balsamic vinegar
1 c. feta cheese, crumbled
2 tbsp. dijon mustard
kosher salt & fresh ground pepper, to taste

- mix it all up
- grill on BBQ or in the oven at 425°F until burgers are perfectly done

MANGO MAYONNAISE

1/2 c. mayonnaise
1 mango, diced
kosher salt & fresh ground pepper, to taste

- in a food processor, *chew it up!*

THEN THE LAYERS...

1 lg. red onion, sliced
8-10 slices of bacon, cook it up
2 slices brie per burger
8-10 spears pickled asparagus
"Mango Mayonnaise" *(see below)*
"Tomato Orange Compote" *(see below)*

So be generous with some gorgeous fresh buns & create a gourmet burger that will have them fall madly in love with you

TOMATO ORANGE COMPOTE

10 tomatoes, diced
2 oranges, sliced
1 md. white onion
1 shallot
4 pickled sliced jalapeno peppers
3 cloves, garlic
handful fresh cilantro
1/2 c. apple cider
1/2 c. brown sugar

- put all fresh ingredients into a deep skillet, on low heat
- bring to a low boil approximately 10min.
- *you can puree or serve as chunky bits... your choice, because life is all about choices*

I'M SWEET, HE'S SOUR, CHICKEN

24 chicken thighs or drumsticks
1 1/2 c. corn starch
1/4 c. butter

- roll chicken in cornstarch and fry in sizzling delightful butter
- transfer chicken over to a casserole dish, when browned on both sides
- meanwhile, make sweet and sour sauce
- pour sauce over chicken
- cover with tinfoil
- bake at 350°F for 45min.
- serve with "Crunchy Rice" *(pg.31)*
- layer with cilantro, fresh peanuts, matchstick carrots and fresh apple pieces
- *delicious!*

SWEET SOUR SAUCE

1 c. sugar
1 c. apple cider vinegar
1/4 c. soy sauce
250 ml. crabapple jelly or orange marmalade

- in a medium saucepan, add sugar, apple cider vinegar, soy sauce, and jelly
- bring to a soft boil, while occasionally stirring

Counter Staple Lemon Loaf
One for eating and one in the freezer... always

1 c. butter
2 c. sugar
5 eggs
lemon zest of 8 lemons (careful to not zest your fingers off)
1 c. lemon juice
1 c. buttermilk
splash Grand Marnier
fresh vanilla bean
3 1/2 c. flour
1 tsp. baking powder
1 tsp. baking soda

- preheat oven at 350°F
- sift flour, baking powder and baking soda in medium bowl, set aside
- mix lemon juice, Grand Marnier and vanilla bean in small bowl and set aside
- cream together butter and sugar until fluffy
- add eggs one at a time until combined, then add your zest
- now like the sandbox, take turns... with buttermilk mixture and flour mixture into the butter until everyone is life long friends
- I use a loaf pan for an extra large loaf... you could split it in two... if you like
- remember to use parchment or grease & flour pans
- bake for 45min. - 1hr.
- **serve with earl grey tea and contentment**

Strawberry Rhubarb Peppercorn Jam

2 c. strawberries, sliced
2 c. rhubarb, sliced
1 c. sugar
big splash raspberry balsamic vinegar
1 tbsp. fresh ground peppercorn

- in a heavy bottomed frying pan cook all ingredients on medium heat
- reduce down into a jam like substance, about 25min.
- **add a pretty spoon…go jammin'**

BLOOMIN' PLUM TURNOVERS

left over "Easy as Pie Pastry" *(pg. 47)*
4 plums, sliced
1 lg. apple, thinly sliced
1/4 c. brown sugar
2 tbsp. butter
splash Chambord
2 tbsp. whipping cream

- saute plums, apples, brown sugar, butter and Chambord, until softened and bubbly
- splash in the whipping cream and cook further for 2min., set aside
- roll out pie pastry and cut into triangle shapes
- spoon bloomin' plums onto triangle, near the longest edge
- roll into crescents
- bake at 375°F for 7-10min.

GRILLY CHEESES FOR THE AM THAT WILL BLOW YOUR MIND

BASIL BRIE GRILL
YIELD 1 SANDWICH

2 slices, fresh favorite bread of choice
handful basil leaves
5 slices fresh brie
5 sm. slices, Lindt sea salt chocolate
handful fresh strawberries

- butter, one side each, of your bread slices
- fill sandwich with ingredients
- using a panini maker, waffle maker or frying pan, *grill the thing… just do it*

APPLEWOOD GRILL

YIELD 1 SANDWICH

2 slices, fresh bread of choice
4 applewood cheese slices
5 thin slices, green apple
4 thin slices, red onion
drizzle wildflower honey
butter

- butter, one side each, of your bread slices
- fill sandwich with ingredients
- using a panini maker, waffle maker or frying pan, grill

BUFFALO MOZZA GRILL
YIELD 1 SANDWICH

2 slices, fresh favorite bread of choice
1 c. leek, white parts, chopped
1 c. button mushrooms, diced
2 eggs
1 tbsp. dijon mustard
4 pieces buffalo mozza
butter

- melt butter in a frying pan
- saute leeks and mushrooms until crispy, set aside
- whisk eggs and dijon mustard
- quickly dip bread into egg mixture
- place onto a cooling rack on a cookie sheet so it is raised
- layer with leeks and mushroom mixture
- quickly dip second slice into egg mixture and place on top
- bake at 425°F for 7min.
- *little cast iron pans are also a great way of cooking these babies up!*

BOAT BAKE

Since acquiring this beautiful **boat** as a gift, I've been looking for a special something to put in it. Naturally, **fantastic** summer faire came to mind. A tremendous amount of king crab legs, fresh cobs of corn with garlic fennel butter, and warmed potato salad. All partnered with grilled skewered strawberries drizzled with balsamic peppercorn reduction. For dessert, my famous raspberry, basil, lemongrass pie offer these guests a simple, yet elegant meal to finish off any **amazing** day.

Stabbed Strawberries with Balsamic Reduction

6 c. strawberries, washed and trimmed
~15 stabbers (skewers)

- stab and grill until medium soft
- *serve to your favorite people only!*

Balsamic Reduction

3/4 c. balsamic vinegar
1/4 c. sugar
fresh ground peppercorn, to taste

- simmer all ingredients until reduced by half

Options:

- add fresh halibut, cut into bite-sized chunks. Alternating with strawberries on skewers

ALL UP IN YOUR GRILL...BOAT?

3 lbs. king crab legs
12 cobs of corn

- heat grill to medium/high temperature
- cook for approx. 20min.
- serve with garlic fennel butter

GARLIC FENNEL BUTTER

1/2 c. butter
1 fennel bulb cored, cleaned and thinly sliced
2 cloves garlic
kosher salt & fresh ground pepper, to taste

- saute gently for 3-4min.
- pour in small dipping bowls

POTATO SIDE OPTIONS:

- "Warmed Potato Salad" *(pg.33)*
- foil-wrapped baked potatoes served with bacon bits, chives, dill and sour cream

RASPBERRY LEMONGRASS PIE
MAKES PEOPLE CRY

4 c. raspberries
1 c. sugar
splash raspberry balsamic
1 tube fresh lemongrass puree (found in the herb section)
2 handfuls basil leaves, chopped
2 c. whipping cream
1/2 c. sugar

- in a deep, heavy-bottomed pot, simmer raspberry balsamic, sugar and 1/2 tube of lemongrass puree until it resembles a jam texture
- add basil
- spoon raspberry filling into pre-prepped pie crust
- bake 15-20min.
- in a bowl, whip together whipping cream and sugar until fluffy
- once pie is cooled, add whipped cream
- *serve and indulge*

EASY AS PIE PASTRY

makes 2 - 9" pie crusts

1 c. butter
2 eggs
splash raspberry balsamic or Grand Marnier
1 vanilla bean, gutted
2 c. flour
1 tsp. baking powder

- in a stand-up mixer with paddle attachment, mix together butter, eggs, raspberry balsamic and vanilla bean guts
- mix in flour and baking powder
- if pastry is still too sticky, add more flour, small amounts at a time, until perfect
- "plunk" dough onto a silpat
- roll out until proper size to fit your pie plate
- add ceramic weights and bake at 375°F for 7-10min.
- let cool

PICK 'EM AND GRAB 'EM PLATTER
FOR KIDLETS 5 YRS. AND UNDER...

beef jerky
handful of Babybel cheese
2 c. sliced bananas
2 pints blueberries
2 pints strawberries
2 c. sliced cucumbers
2 c. grape tomatoes
sm. cups of flavoured yogurt

- create a collage of food folly, mixed with toys and items to fit the theme of your gathering

FOOD SWAG
TEENAGERS DIG THIS!

popcorn
craisins
peanuts
goldfish crackers
cheerios
chocolate-covered almonds
cheezies

- in the coolest bowl you can find, add a shwack-load of this stuff... don't be shy!
- **use the leftovers for lunches and snacks in the car**

CHOCOLATE COVERED CHIPS

1 lg. bag of kettle-cooked salt and vinegar chips
1/2 c. high-quality milk chocolate (such as Bernard Callebault or Lindt)

- melt chocolate in a double boiler
- place chips on a super nifty platter
- drizzle chocolate over chips **until your heart is content**

cozy pig tubes

1 mild Italian Spolumbo's sausage per guest
fresh bakery buns
~ 2 c. balsamic onions *(see below)*
3-4 red jalapenos per guest
2-3 c. mixed cheeses, such as jack and cheddar
1 c. "You're such an Aioli" sauce *(see below)*

- grill up your "pig tubes"
- cozy them up in a bun with all the layers you desire
- ***be generous, open your heart, and good things will come your way***

balsamic onions

3 red onions
1/4 c. butter
2 tbsp. Mirabello balsamic vinegar

- saute butter and onions at medium heat until soft
- increase heat, add balsamic vinegar, saute for an additional 2 min.
- ***finished!***

"you're such an aioli" sauce

1 c. mayonnaise
juice from half of a lemon
1 tbsp. capers (optional)
2 scallions, white and green parts
pinch of kosher salt & fresh ground pepper

- whisk all ingredients until well mixed

sweet taters

2 lg. sweet potatoes
2-3 c. canola oil
3 tbsp. rosemary
kosher salt & fresh ground pepper, to taste

- preheat oil in a deep frying pan to 375°F on a candy thermometer
- cut sweet potatoes into fry-sized pieces
- deep fry until crispy and golden
- transfer to a paper towel covered plate to remove excess oil
- pop into a bowl and toss with rosemary, salt and pepper
- serve with extra "You're Such an Aioli" sauce

VANILLA BEAN COTTON CLOUD CAKE

* read this… in its entirety…immediately

2 c. sugar, pulsed in food processor until fine
1 1/3 c. sifted cake flour
12-14 egg whites
2 tsp. cream of tartar
2 vanilla bean pods, gutted
splash of Grand Marnier
1/2 c. grated milk chocolate (Bernard Callebaut)

- preheat oven to 350°F
- grab a coffee… this one takes a bit
- in a pail, combine 1/2 c. sugar with flour, sift four times and set aside
- after you are a bit mental from separating eggs, beat them on high speed until peaks are firm
- reduce speed to medium, add remaining 1 1/2 c. sugar
- beat until lustrous
- add vanilla bean guts and Grand Marnier, continue to mix on low speed
- now hang on… its gonna get a little funky
- scrape egg whites into a large bowl
- take a quarter of the flour/sugar mixture. Sift again into the bowl until all flour is gone, while *folding* ingredients together. **NO STIRRING!**
- fold chocolate into mixture
- find yourself a greased, cocoa-powdered bundt pan. Pour ingredients in
- bake 35-45min. until cake springs back to touch

OPTIONS:

- wrap loonies and toonies in tinfoil and add to batter to create a classic money cake

COTTON CLOUD GLAZE

2 c. chopped white chocolate
1/3 c. grated orange peel
3/4 c. whipping cream

- put all ingredients in a heat proof bowl and double-boil this baby down
- drizzle on top of cooled "Vanilla Bean Cotton Cloud Cake"

Boozy Strawberry Choco"Latte" Cake
...with Caramelized Bacon Bits

2 c. flour
2 tsp. baking soda
1/2 tsp. baking powder
1 c. chopped chocolate, semi-sweet
1/2 c. butter
2 c. packed brown sugar
3 eggs
1 vanilla bean pod, emasculated
3/4 c. sour cream
1/2 c. brewed espresso
1/2 c. coffee liqueur (Kahlua)
1 c. whipping cream

- preheat oven to 350°F
- grease and cocoa-powder two round pans
- in a pail, mix flour, baking soda, and baking powder. Set aside
- melt chocolate in a double boiler, let cool, add vanilla bean
- in mixer, beat butter, sugar, and eggs until fluffy
- in another bowl, mix sour cream, espresso, and coffee liqueur
- now the grand finale… at low speed in mixer, alternate flour mixture, sour cream mixture and chocolate in fourths, scraping down sides as you go
- mix until all ingredients are well combined
- poor batter into pans
- bake for 30-35min.
- let cool, give yourself a hug… homemade cakes are filled with "lovey" goodness
- layer with "I Love the Middle", "Strawberry Balsamic Jam" and "Whipping Cream", "Boozy Frosted Bits" and "Caramelized Bacon"
- *decorate this masterpiece with great thought and creativity*

"I Love the Middle"
Strawberry Balsamic Jam

3 c. cleaned strawberries
1/2 c. balsamic vinegar
1 c. white sugar

- reduce over medium heat for approx. 30min.

Whipping Cream

1 c. whipping cream
2 tbsp. maple syrup
dash of cinnamon

- *whip it...whip it good!*

Boozy Frosty Bits

1 1/2 c. chocolate chips
3/4 c. chilled sour cream
1 tbsp. coffee liqueur

- melt chocolate chips with coffee liqueur in a double boiler
- whisk in sour cream until desired texture
- spread on cake

Caramelized Bacon

10 strips of bacon, cut into bite-sized pieces
1/2 c. white sugar

- saute bacon on medium-high heat until golden brown
- add sugar, watch as it caramelizes... don't overcook! Chill on parchment paper.
- sprinkle on top of cake

RAZZLE DAZZLE

Your children's toy box is the best place to find cake toppers and decorative charms to play with in a creative and cost-effective way. I've used everything from Spiderman to dump trucks to bakugan, and of course, **Lego**. Look for interesting pieces throughout the year before you throw away toys. Think of them in a new and exciting way and keep a small box of these treasures for future use. For girls, I love jewelry, **cool** boxes filled with a special surprise, great candy, crafting materials with a feminine touch. Basically, just be open to experiencing preparation differently to your celebrations… stay away from the party aisles!

If purchasing cupcakes from your local bakery consider adding some flare with edible spray, super cool candles and other fancy **baubles**. Some of my more clever ideas include napkin ring holders as a vase for fresh flowers on top, old bracelets for sparkle. Even old rings can add **"razzle dazzle"**. Have fun, enjoy being different... permission granted!

AUTUMN
"WITH THE WARMTH OF THE FIRE, THEY ARRIVE"

WARMED CHOCOLATE LOVE IN A CUP

2 c. Bernard Callebaut milk chocolate
1 c. whipped cream
splash of half & half cream
1 tsp. cinnamon
1/2 tsp. chili flakes
1 pod, vanilla bean

- warm all ingredients at a low heat
- serve with vanilla ice cream or fresh whipped cream

Upon walking into the Volio household, I felt immediately overwhelmed with an abundancy of warmth, love, and acceptance. The atmosphere of this beautiful home instantly makes anyone who walks in feel a sense of security. Not to mention the beautiful family that takes anyone in with open arms. We are truly blessed to have the friends, family, and wonderful moments in this house that we may keep as beautiful memories.

Michaela Trent

LOVES THEY COME

Sometimes as many as **22** teenagers will infiltrate my home at a moment's notice. As ravenous for food as they are for good conversation, these peeps hold a **special** place in the fibers of my heart: gracious guests who **adore** fantastic ingredients, the opportunity to cook, and the occasional off-coloured joke. With the laughter and adoration from the gobbling guests, we all emerge from these gatherings **full** in many ways.

Karamel Apple Babies

I don't make my own caramel for these heavenly "Karamel Apple Babies". I buy Kraft caramel squares and add a splash of whipping cream... so the thickness remains.

- get yourself some fancy skewer sticks, some gorgeous ladies and gent's and dip away
- design beautifully
- *serve with a cheeky grin*

YUMMY

FRIENDSHIPS

As the **masculine** and **feminine** energies collide in my kitchen, I find myself fascinated by the precision of the knife work of the men. Billy, in particular, has the mad skills of a **chef**, surprising even himself with his **prowess**.

Remaining connected with the teenagers requires an ability to feed the masses, while also remaining a shadow in the background. Whilst hopefully imparting some earthly **wisdom** without them thinking you are a total **dork**!

ROASTED SUNDAY CHICKEN

whole raw chicken
1 apple, cut into pieces
5 whole garlic bulbs
1 whole shallot
handful of fresh herbs (*ie.* rosemary, cilantro, dill or oregano)
2 tbsp. butter
kosher salt & fresh ground pepper, to taste

- in a roasting pan, stuff the sweet bird with apple pieces, garlic, shallot and fresh herbs
- smother bird with butter
- add salt and pepper to taste
- roast at 450°F for 1 1/2hrs. uncovered
- transfer from oven to platter and serve to gracious guests
- save all juices from roasting pan

"Cheeky Cheesy Chicky" Poutine

remaining chicken from "Sunday Dinner", chopped up
"Crispy Fry Wedges" *(pg 71)*
"C.C.C. Sauce" *(see below)*
2 pkgs. cheese curds (I find mine @ Costco)
handful fresh dill
fresh ground pepper

- fill handled bowls/cups with fries
- mix chicken, sauce, cheese curds, dill, and pepper together in the dish until melted
- ***serve immediately***

C.C.C. Sauce

chicken juices (from "Sunday Dinner")
4 c. chicken broth
2 tbsp. butter
1/4 c. flour

- melt butter and add flour to create a roux to thicken sauce, set aside
- in a deep pan, mix chicken juices and broth, whisk gently.
- add roux and whisk until well mixed

CRISPY FRY WEDGES

5-6 russet potatoes

- cut potatoes into wedges
- heat canola oil until it comes to a quiet, rumbling boil
- using a basketed/slotted spoon, drop fries into oil
- cook until crispy and browned
- remove and drain on paper-toweled plate
- add "C.C.C. Sauce" *(pg. 70)*
- ***brilliant!***

TOPPING OPTIONS:

tomatoes
- jalapenos
- sour cream
- salsa
- sauteed corn
- black beans
- avocado
- cilantro
- green onions

OH HELLO! TACO IN A BAG

2 lbs. local lean ground beef
1/4 c. chili powder
1 white onion
1 yellow pepper
1 orange pepper
1-2 c. grated monterey jack cheese

- buy yourself a box of individually sized bags of nacho chips
- saute onions and peppers in pan until soft on medium heat
- add beef and chili powder, cook until no longer pink
- cut bags open on the long side to create a bowl effect
- get your guests to crunch their chips into small pieces
- throw beef and cheese into bag, add toppings of your choice

DON'T BE A BAG... MAKE A LUNCH

I'll never forget my own school **dayz**, watching the beautiful Ivana pull out her brown paper sack of mouth watering, jealous-driven delight. **Homemade** croissant sandwiches, cookies, fruit, special handmade treats, as I sat empty handed and sooooo hungry. She's lucky I didn't jump her in the hallway for that **amaze-delicio-tastic** brown paper bag. So cheers to all these lovely ideas, and Ivana, wherever you are, I bet you are now making those **scrumptio** lunches for your children.

POP... AND IT'S OVER

1 1/2 c. half & half cream, warmed
4 eggs
1 c. flour
1/2 c. **hot** butter or beef drippings (split equally between batter and pan)

- pre-heat oven to 425°F
- in a stand up mixer, mix cream, eggs, fat, & flour
- heat pan with fat prior to pouring in the batter
- bake for 30min. *or until as big as your head*

CREPES

4 eggs
1 c. flour
1 c. milk, warmed
1/4 c h2o
2 tbsp. melted butter
lemon/orange zest

- blend egg, flour and butter
- add milk, h2o and zest

CREPE OPTIONS:
- full banana, peanut butter and a honey comb
- Nutella and fresh strawberries

POP-OVER OPTIONS:
- roast beef, horseradish, mayo, fresh basil, havarti cheese and a pickled asparagus, on the side
- chicken, thinly sliced apple, red onion, cranberry sauce and mayo

SANDWICH OPTIONS:
- tuna salad; with sliced fennel bulb, pickled jalapenos, scallions, garlic, mayo, splash of jalapeno juice and coarse pepper
- egg salad; with green onions, fresh dill, dill pickles, splash of pickle juice, dijon mustard, mayo, salt and pepper
- frozen sandwich; meat and cheese of your choice, mustard and mayo. Wrap in paper towel, pop in a freezer bag and freeze until needed

DROPS OF CHOCO-COCOA-NUT
AKA ELLE'S PROTEIN BALLS

1/2 c. brown sugar
1/2 c. butter
1/2 c. half & half cream
3 c. rolled oats
6 tbsp. Bernard Callebaut cocoa
1 c. coconut
1 vanilla bean, flesh only
white chocolate, for drizzling

- over medium heat, bring brown sugar, butter and cream to a bubbly boil
- remove from heat and add rolled oats, cocoa, coconut and vanilla bean flesh
- drop onto parchment paper, set in fridge or outside to cool
- *drizzle with a little bit of white chocolate for beautiness*

PROTEIN BALL OPTION

1/4 c. nutritional yeast
1/4 c. coconut

- form into ball & roll in ingredients
- place balls into fridge, leave uncovered
- *the harder they get, the better they taste… wink wink*

GOBBLE GOBBLE

Perfecting a **turkey** dinner is no small feat. There is a lot of pre-prep required to pull this off without the cook feeling stressed to the **max**. Some of my secrets are to pre-make sweet potatoes, a brussel sprout dish, and pastry for pies up to 2 weeks prior. Put together your cranberry compote 3-4 days before the big meal...

Create soup 2 days before and refrigerate. Then, on the eve of turkey day, pull everything out to defrost. All you have left to do is make your pies, saute up your stuffing, pop in **"Gobble Gobble"** and peel potatoes. Go outside at this point with a beverage of your choice to where a raging fire awaits and a roasted apple **feast** commences with the people you tend to do these "family" meals with. After apples have been enjoyed, drag guests' sweet bottoms up into the kitchen to warm up for the rest of the meal. Make gravy, set your table and give **thanks**... for all is well!

Using the outdoors for entertaining in the cooler temperatures can be a challenge. Fall is chilly in the **wild wild west**, but I keep my outdoor room with a big outdoor fireplace and loads of **blankets** on hand until after Thanksgiving.

Roasting apples on a fire for an appetizer is pure, **rustic** heaven. Hand guests a big mug of soup, a blanket, and away they go. **Comforted** and **warm** from the inside out!

MMM ROASTED APPLES

1 apple per guest

- wrap in tinfoil, roast for 15min. on low-ember burning fire
- I love using a cast iron pan for each guest to unwrap their apple into
- coat with butter, brown sugar and cinnamon
- *scrump~diddly~umptious!*

I'm almost as wild as this... Mushroom Soup
my son in law... Ali's favourite

1 1/2 c. portobello mushrooms, chopped
1 1/2 c. shiitake mushrooms, chopped
1 c. white button mushrooms, chopped
2 c. leeks (white part only), diced
1 c. spanish onion, diced
1/2 c. butter
splash avocado oil
1/4 c. flour
1 c. white wine
1/2 c. heavy cream
6-8 c. chicken broth
fresh thyme - 3 sprigs + 2 tbsp. leaves
kosher salt & fresh ground pepper, to taste

- in a large frying pan, add butter and avocado oil
- fry mushrooms, leeks, and onions until moisture is minimal (about 15-20min.) while continually scraping the bottom to loosen up all the flavour magic
- ok, people... turn down the heat to medium, add flour, muck it around and scraping that bottom for approx. 1min.
- douse all that fungi with white wine, scraping and messing around
- add chicken broth
- reduce heat to low-medium, add thyme sprigs and simmer for approx. 20min.
- add salt, pepper, fresh thyme leaves and cream as you serve in beautiful mugs for a change
- *scrumptio!*

AUTUMN SOUP

3 leeks (white part only) cleaned & sliced
1 white onion, sliced
3 md. sweet potatoes, diced
3 md. potatoes, diced
6 c. chicken broth
1/2 c. half 'n half cream
handful of fresh herbs
smidge of "Caramelized Bacon" *(pg.56)*

- on medium heat, in a medium pot, saute leeks and onion until softened
- add chicken broth, sweet potato, and potato. Cook until tender
- using a food processor, puree soup to desired consistency
- return to soup pot and add cream
- *serve straight away with a cocked eyebrow, fresh herbs and "Caramelized Bacon"*

dOn't be a turkey... Dinner

(rule of thumb is 20min./lb.)

1 fresh turkey
"Freaking Fantastic Stuffing" (*pg.85*)
butter (be generous)
kosher salt & fresh ground pepper, to taste

- open that bird cavity and defile it with the delicious bread bits
- tie closed with string if you like, I never do
- coat gobble-gobble in butter, salt, and pepper
- pop into a mother-huge roasting pan that you bought special for the day, uncovered, and cook away... 30min. at 400°F, then turn down to 375°F
- remove turkey from pan, cover and let rest on a platter
- set aside roasting pan and its juices for "Giblet Gravy" (*pg.84*)

GIBLET GRAVY

1/4 c. flour
1/4 c. butter, melted
1 c. chicken broth
1/2 c. white wine
2 cloves garlic, chopped
2 tbsp. rosemary, chopped
2 tbsp. apple jelly
kosher salt & fresh ground pepper, to taste
giblets (optional)

- in a bowl, mix flour and butter to create a roux, set aside
- with a whisk, loosen up precious bits from bottom of pan
- add remaining ingredients while continuing to whisk away
- bring to a slow rumble and cook until well combined
- add roux and cook until desired thickness is achieved

FREAKING FANTASTIC STUFFING

5 c. bread cubes (jalapeno cheese bread, corn bread, sundried tomato bread or anything else other than everyday bread)
1 lg. onion
1 c. butter (more if needed)
1 c. chopped hazelnuts
1 c. chopped apple
fresh thyme
fresh oregano
2 tbsp. orange zest
kosher salt & fresh ground pepper, to taste

- in a large pot, melt butter over medium heat
- toss in nuts, apple, and onion. Saute until softened
- add bread cubes and cook for about 10min., stirring occasionally to make sure bread gets soft from soaking in the butter
- remove from heat, add fresh herbs, salt and pepper

WHIPPED POTATOES

10-12 red potatoes, peeled
1 c. half & half cream
1/4 c. butter
1 c. fontina cheese
kosher salt & fresh ground pepper, to taste

- cook potatoes until soft, not mushy
- add cream
- with a hand mixer, whip those babies
- mix in butter, fontina cheese, salt and pepper
- *serve hot*

MAPLE INFUSED YAMS
people will whisper about this behind your back

4 lg. yams, cut into bite sized chunks
3/4 c. great Canadian maple syrup
1/2 c. butter
1/3 c. flour
1/3 c. brown sugar
1/2 c. coarsely chopped pecans

- put yams into a pot of water, boil until tender
- drain and set aside in a nice rectangular baking dish that can also be used for serving... kills two birds with one stone
- now take your syrup and pour it lovingly over the yams
- in a small mixing bowl mix flour, brown sugar and pecans
- cut in butter with a bread knife until it resembles a coarse meal
- sprinkle with intention
- bake at 350°F for 25min.
- *totes ma goats*

B.B.B.S.
(Bacon, Balsamic, Brussel Sprouts)

12 slices of harvest bacon
4 c. brussel sprouts, cleaned, halved and trimmed
1/2 c. h2o
1/4 c. Mirabello balsamic vinegar
4 tbsp. butter

- in a large pan, cook up your bacon until just crispy
- with a slotted spoon, remove bacon onto a paper-toweled plate
- put brussel into the pan with the bacon fat, tossing about until brussels start to brown
- add h2o, cover and further cook 4-5min.
- add balsamic on a medium heat, reduce vinegar until it looks syrupy
- turn heat to low
- add butter, bacon and salt and pepper
- *voila!*

Fresh Figgy Cranberry Compote

1 c. h2o
1 12oz. bag cranberries
1 c. sugar
1 c. dried figs or dates
1 granny smith apple
juice and zest from 2 mandarin oranges

- cook water, berries and sugar in a sauce pan over low heat until berries "pop"
- add figs, apples, mandarin zest and juice
- cook for another 15min. or so until compote seems nicely thickened, set aside and let cool completely
- find yourself a super sexy jar to put it all in
- use the leftovers for serving with lamb pops or chicken dishes for the next few weeks. I even like it on pancakes *(crazy, I know)*

CHOCOLATE PUMPKIN PIE

1 "Easy as Pie Pastry" *(pg.47)*
1 can (796 ml) pumpkin pie filling
1 c. Bernard Callebaut chocolate, melted

- pre-cook pie shell at 450°F for 7min.
- follow pumpkin pie instructions on can for filling
- remove crust from oven, add filling and drizzle chocolate in a circular pattern
- bake at 350°F for 30min. for shallow pies and 40-45min. for deep pies

WHIPPED CREAM

2 c. whipping cream
2 tbsp. maple syrup
splash cinnamon

- whip all ingredients until fluffy

Cozy, Comfort Foods for Any Time

FRENCH KISSED ONION SOUP

4 Spanish onions
4 garlic cloves
4 sprigs thyme or rosemary
1/4 c. butter
splash cooking oil
1/4 c. flour
1 c. port
6 c. beef broth
2 c. Gruyère cheese

- saute onions and garlic on medium heat until soft
- add flour, scraping bottom as you mix about
- add port, continue to saute until floury mixture is combined
- add broth, stir until soup looks cohesive
- simmer 20min.
- put into bowls of choice, top with cheese
- broil until cheese is browned
- serve with fresh bread on the side…

I don't do soggy bits!

Beef Tenderloin Roast

1 beef roast (size depending on number of guests)
butter
kosher salt & freshly ground pepper, to taste

- place roast into deep roasting pan
- slather hunky piece of meat with butter
- season with generous amounts of salt and pepper
- DO NOT COVER
- cook at 450°F for 1hr. 15min. until medium rare
- *crack a window... its gonna get a little smoky*

Horsey Mayo

2 shallots
1 c. mayonnaise
2 tbsp. horseradish

- mix and spread onto buns

BOY BEEFY DIP

beef tenderloin roast, sliced to desired thickness
"Dippity Doo" *(see below)*
"Balsamic Onions" *(pg.53)*
"Horsey Mayo" *(pg.93)*
choice buns

- once cooked, remove roast from pan and place onto cutting board, cover with tinfoil, and let nap
- in the meantime... make "Dippity Doo", "Balsamic Onions", and "Horsey Mayo"
- serve beef on buns of choice (spread with "Horsey Mayo"), with "Balsamic Onions", and a side of "Dippity Doo"
- *say no more!*

DIPPITY DOO

8 c. beef broth
4 tbsp. horseradish
4 tbsp. rosemary
massive splash red wine

- heat ingredients of roasting pan on stove top with beef broth, horseradish, rosemary and red wine on medium heat until it rumbles to a low boil
- whisk to loosen bits from the bottom of the roasting pan
- add sliced beef to keep warm *until hungry hippos arrive*

I like your rack... of lamb

rack of lamb (cut into lamb pop segments)
"Saucy Sauce" *(see below)*
"Crusty Top" *(see below)*

- preheat oven to 425°F
- apply "Saucy Sauce" with a pastry brush, generously
- roll your rack in "Crusty Top" until covered
- place on a cooling rack on a cookie sheet
- take the rack, on the rack, and put it in the oven
- cook to desired temperature
- *serve with reduction and a big goblet of wine, and remember - don't give away the farm*

Brothy Balsamic Reduction

1 tbsp. avocado oil
2 shallots, chopped
1/3 c. Mirabello balsamic vinegar
3/4 c. chicken broth
1 tbsp. butter

- on medium heat, saute oil and shallots approx. 30sec.
- add balsamic vinegar, reduce for 1min.
- add chicken broth, reduce by half, 3-5min.
- remove from heat
- add butter
- *serve in a pretty little bowl on the side*

Crusty Top

2 handfuls bread crust
handful of basil, cilantro and rosemary mix
2 cloves garlic
2 tbsp. oil
kosher salt & fresh ground pepper, to taste

- chop all this up in your "pushy buttony thingy" (food processor)
- transfer to a flat dish, set aside

Saucy Sauce

1/4 c. mayonnaise
2 tbsp. dijon mustard
splash Mirabello balsamic vinegar
kosher salt & fresh ground pepper

- mix all ingredients together, set aside

pork me Jack (apples)

3 tbsp. oil
pork chops (1 per person)
3 tbsp. butter
3 apples, sliced
1 tbsp. cinnamon
1/2 c. brown sugar
big splash Jack Daniel's
1 lighter

- pre-heat oven to 425°F
- on high heat, in a deep skillet, add oil and sear pork chops on each side
- transfer to a raised rack on a cookie sheet, keep skillet aside
- finish off in oven 5-7min.
- on medium heat, melt butter in a skillet
- add apple slices and saute for approx. 3-5min.
- add cinnamon, brown sugar, cook down for 1min.
- grab an audience - things are about to get fiery
- splash in the Jack Daniel's and light it on fire... safely, of course
- serve with your choice of carbs

BREAKFAST DOUGH-NUGGETS

1 c. unsalted butter
1/2 c. maple syrup
1 c. h2o
8 eggs
2 1/2 c. flour
canola oil

- in a saucepan, add butter, maple syrup and water, bring to a boil and then take off of heat
- add flour, return to low heat and cook until ball forms
- transfer to a medium bowl, and mix in eggs one at a time, with a hand mixer
- fill a pot with canola oil until approximately 3" deep and heat to 350°F using a candy thermometer. Keep thermometer in pot throughout to ensure oil remains at proper temperature or dough-nuggets can get funky
- drop dough into oil, cook until browned
- serve with chocolate sauce or blended strawberries with icing sugar and orange zest
- *try to not eat 500!!!*

Maple Marnier Bouillie with Brown Sugar

2 tbsp. Grand Marnier
2 tbsp. maple syrup
2 c. milk
1 c. porridge
2 fresh bananas, no brown bits, sliced
splash half 'n half cream
tinch brown sugar

- in a medium saucepan, add Grand Marnier, maple syrup, milk, and porridge
- bring to a boil over medium heat
- serve with fresh banana slices, cream and brown sugar

Smoked Oyster & Quail Egg Benedict
if you say so

1/2 c. butter, melted
3 egg yolks (standard eggs)
2 tbsp lemon juice
kosher salt & fresh ground pepper, to taste
fresh baguette slices or standard english muffins
2 cans smoked oysters
1 dozen quail eggs
12 slices traditional back bacon

- in food processor, add melted butter, egg yolks, lemon juice, pepper and salt, and mix this heart stopper all up
- cook up quail eggs and bacon
- toast and butter both sides of baguette slices/english muffins
- now layer it all up. I like oysters on top - it's a surprise and so flippin' tasteeee
- serve with "Stewed Tomato White Bean Compote" *(see below)*

Stewed Tomato White Bean Compote

1 lg. can diced tomatoes
1 can white kidney beans, drained and rinsed
1 sm. white onion
handful basil leaves
splash Mirabello balsamic vinegar

- in a medium saucepan over medium heat, warm all ingredients until bubbly
- serve in a small little pot with your smoked oyster bene *and your guests will never leave*

BAKED PUMPKIN SLICE WITH COFFEE YOGURT

1 slice pumpkin per person
brown sugar
cinnamon
1 dollop whipped cream per person
1/2 c. coffee yogurt per person

- sprinkle pumpkin slices with brown sugar and cinnamon
- bake at 450°F until tender
- serve with whipped cream and yogurt...
and a smile!

STUFFED DOUGH
DEEP DISH PAN, PEOPLE, BUY ONE!

3 c. bread flour
3 tsp. kosher salt
2 1/2 tsp. dried active yeast
2 1/2 tsp. honey or sugar
10 oz. lukewarm water
3 tbsp. extra virgin olive oil

- in mixing bowl, whisk together flour and salt
- in separate bowl, add dried active yeast and honey to water
- when the water/yeast/sugar has proofed (approx 5min.), add oil into bowl with flour
- mix until you've formed a moist dough ball and all flour is incorporated. Note: add flour as required if too wet/sticky, and/or add water if too dry
- pour dough ball out onto flat surface, and knead for 5min., adding flour as required, until you've formed a semi-moist smooth dough ball
- dust dough ball with flour and place back into mixing bowl
- cover bowl with a damp kitchen towel, to double in size
- place dough onto a lightly floured surface and break into 4 equal-sized dough balls

TOMATO SAUCE

per pizza:
1 28 oz. can of "6-in-1 tomatoes"
1 tbsp. of extra virgin olive oil
1 tsp. kosher salt
2 tbsp. chopped fresh oregano
2 tbsp. chopped fresh basil

- mix all ingredients together in a bowl

THIN CRUST DOUGH

makes four 12" thin crust

4 c. bread flour
4 tsp. kosher salt
3 tsp. dried active yeast
3 tsp. honey or sugar
16 oz. lukewarm water

- in a mixing bowl, whisk together flour and salt
- in a separate small bowl, add yeast and honey to water
- when the water/yeast/sugar has proofed (approx. 5min.), pour into mixing bowl with flour
- mix by hand until dough ball is formed and all flour incorporated. Note: add flour as required if too sticky, and/or add water if too dry
- pour dough ball out onto lightly floured surface, and knead 5min., adding flour as required, until you've formed a semi-moist smooth dough ball.
- dust dough ball with flour and place back into mixing bowl to double in size
- pour dough onto lightly floured surface and break into 4 equal-sized dough balls, cover until use
- hand stretch the dough (gently), popping large air bubbles, and then roll out into a circle, approx. 1/8" thick
- pour finely ground cornmeal onto silpat
- place stretched dough onto silpat
- cut edges if hanging over sides to form a circle, or optionally, fold edges to form a crust

STUFFED PIZZA

"Stuffed Dough" *(pg.101)*
6 c. low moisture part-skim mozzarella, shredded
250 g. med. Italian pork sausage
2 tbsp. fennel seeds
finely grated parmesan cheese

- pre-heat oven to 475°F
- add fennel seeds to sausage, roll into marble-sized balls
- split dough ball into two balls, one 3/4 and the other 1/4 of the original. Place the smaller ball back into mixing bowl and cover
- hand stretch the dough (gently), popping large air bubbles, and then roll out into a circle, approx. 1/8" thick
- lightly oil a deep dish pizza pan - pan should be 2" high around sides
- place stretched dough onto the pan, should just barely hang over the side
- flatten/smooth dough where needed
- place raw sausage onto dough
- cover with cheese
- place pan aside
- stretch small ball gently, roll out until paper-thin
- place dough on top of deep dish pan
- fold both dough layers together to seal
- pour sauce on top
- make two slits on top of pizza to release air
- turn oven temp. to 450°F and cook on middle rack 30-35min. until crust is browned
- remove from oven, let pizza rest for 5min.
- sprinkle with finely grated parmesan
- *cut and serve with verve*

Caramelized Onion Zzaaa

2 red onions, thinly sliced
3 tbsp. butter
1/2 c. goat cheese
"Thin Crust Dough" *(pg.102)*
olive/avocado oil

- saute onions and butter until soft, set aside
- on prepared dough, drizzle your choice of oil
- add sauteed onions and pea-sized drops of goat cheese
- gently place onto pre-heated stone in oven
- cook 8-10min. at 550°F, or 10-12min. at 500°F until crust is golden brown

BASIL BUFFALO MOZZAAA

15 slices buffalo mozza, thin as possible
handful basil
"Thin Crust Dough" *(pg.102)*
"Tomato Sauce" *(pg.101)*

- drizzle oil and ladle sauce onto prepped dough
- add toppings
- gently place onto preheated stone in oven
- cook 8-10min. at 550°F, or 10-12min. at 500°F until crust is golden brown

Other zzaaa Options:

- arugula tossed in Mirabello balsamic vinegar, oil, kosher salt & fresh ground pepper
- basil pesto
- olives
- artichokes
- bocconcini cheese or other bold choices
- herb combos that excite
- jalapenos

WINTER

"REKINDLE THE LOVE, THE HOPE, THE JOY, THE MAGIC"

CHRISTMAS FOREST

In this Christmas **cocoon**... all is well. Santa letters are in the red mailbox and we are drawn in to read stories of holiday folklore in amongst the trees. Snuggled up with the glorious smell of these branches, we are indeed reminded that this is not a dream. Our Christmas home is where our gratitude lies as we **ReKindle**: the **hope**, the **joy**, the **magic** and the **love** that is bursting out of our finest Christmas seams.

THE BELL...

Many a child has erupted into a state of giggly **exuberance** upon entering the Christmas forest. Teenagers sleep in it, toddlers play in it. I, of course, play and occasionally rest in it. But my favourite thing of all is to read **"The Polar Express"**

Slipping a **bell** privately into a chosen child's pocket... then at the end of the story the pure delight created when they find the **magic** bell is quite **magnificent**. Unless it's my children... they just shake their heads.

DECADENCE

BABES + BISCOTTI

I do it every year. Guest lists vary from my son's volleyball team to the new **friendships** that found us throughout the year, and always, the tried-and-trued **kindred** souls that fill my life with love and kindness. Baking together, sharing a drink and some great food, as the home of Christmas surrounds us in a blanket of warmth. I am quietly reminded why I do what I do for these few brief hours. We are released into a place of Christmas **bliss**, deeply content to breathe in the aroma of each yummy scent... to just **be!!!**

CRANBERRY WHITE CHOCOLATE BISCOTTI
MAKE FOR AM COFFEE DATES WITH LOVES OF YOUR LIFE

2 1/2 c. flour
1 tsp. baking powder
1 1/2 c. sugar
1 tsp. Grand Marnier
1/2 c. unsalted butter
2 lg. eggs
1 1/2 c. dried cranberries
1 1/2 c. chopped white chocolate
2 egg whites, whisked until foamy

- with great Christmas gusto, in a stand up mixer, beat sugar, butter, eggs and Grand Marnier
- in your flour pail, combine flour and baking powder
- add flour mix to butter concoction and stir about. Continue to engage until fully incorporated
- dump dough onto silpat with extra flour nearby, divide into two and shape into nice square logs
- put onto cookie sheets and with great intention, using a pastry brush, apply egg whites on top
- melt white chocolate in a double boiler, set aside
- bake at 350°F for 25min.
- remove, let cool and cut into biscotti pieces, put back into oven to brown cut sides and remove again to cool
- drizzle with white chocolate
- *take a bite*

SPARKLY SNOWFLAKE SWEETIES
FOR THE TREE OR A CUP OF TEA

2 1/2 c. flour
1/2 tsp. baking powder
2 tbsp. freshly grated orange zest
1 c. unsalted butter
1 1/4. c sugar
1 egg
1 tsp. Grand Marnier

- in stand up mixer, joyfully add butter, sugar, egg, Grand Marnier and orange zest
- spin 'er up until fluffy and stuff
- in flour pail, mix baking powder and flour, then add to butter mixture
- combine nicely and wrap in plastic and pop into fridge for about 30min.
- when ready to play, roll out on floured silpat
- buy a stunning snowflake cookie cutter - I love my copper one
- bake at 350°F for 10-12min.
- let cool and decorate

CREATIVE IDEAS:
- gold, silver and copper paint
- edible sparkles in different colours, shapes and sizes
- keep your eyes open for any idea-evoking items throughout the year

The pure **elegance** of this day: chatting away, baking biscotti and gorgeous snowflake cookies, all with the soul **intention** of designing a beautiful gift box for my guests to take home. **Surprise**... its simply that time of the year.

WHIMSICAL

Satisfying the holiday appetites of my working **"elf"** friends gives me great frosty delight. These are **cheat** days worth waiting for. So sit back and enjoy a bite with us. Bring your **wreathy** grin.

Lovely Layers, Like You've Never Seen Before

1st Layer - The Brown

1 pkg. fresh, local ground lamb
1 pkg. fresh, ground beef
2 tbsp. chili powder
2 tbsp. garlic powder
2 tbsp. garlic salt

- saute until cooked thoroughly
- set aside

2nd Layer - The Berry

2 c. blueberries & blackberries
1/2 c. sugar
big splash of cognac

- cook on medium heat until reduced to a jam-like consistency
- set aside

3rd Layer - The Cream

1 can white kidney beans
2 tbsp. fresh rosemary
2 cloves garlic
splash Mirabello balsamic vinegar

- put in food processor and pulverize those bits until lovely and creamy
- add h2o as necessary, so its not too pasty
- set aside

4th Layer - The Green

4 avocados, pitted and scooped
1 lemon
6 pickled jalapeños, diced

- mix until a guacamole mixture is achieved
- set aside

5th Layer - The Toppings

1 container sour cream
1 c. fresh pomegranate
handful fresh cilantro

- okay, clever folks. In a clear glass bowl start with "1st Layer - the Brown". Spread it evenly like you mean it, then work your way to the "5th Layer - the Toppings"
- now grab your crackers, chips, or homemade pita crisps - *whatever floats your newly layered boat!*

Sticky Nikki's Gooey Mess

1 wheel, double cream brie
5 figs, sliced
1/3 c. wild rose honey
1/3 c. Mirabello balsamic vinegar

- drizzle honey and vinegar over brie, cover in figs, pop into oven
- bake at 400°F until gooey mess is achieved
- serve warm with creative cracker choices

Options:

- toasted pecans, served on a bed of arugula with buttery toasts

GINGER, WHAT KINDA CAKE DID YOU SAY?!

2 c. flour
1 tsp. baking soda
1 tsp. ground ginger
2 tsp. cinnamon
1/2 tsp. cloves
1/2 tsp. allspice
1 c. brown sugar
1 lg. egg
1/4 c. canola oil
1 can pumpkin puree
1/2 c. plain yogurt
1/4 c. "moles-asses" (molasses)
splash of Jack Daniels

- go to it...
- preheat oven to 375°F
- in a large stand up mixer, beat sugar, oil, and egg... continue with pumpkin, yogurt, molasses, and Jack Daniels, mix
- add flour mixture, mix
- pour batter into greased pan of your choice. I use little individual gingerbread pans for kids, cake pan for big kids
- drizzle with caramel, hazelnuts, ice cream
- ***own the fact that "you got this"***

sexy caramel

1/3 c. h2o
1 1/2 c. sugar
1 1/4 c. heavy cream
vanilla bean (optional)

- in a medium, heavy-bottomed, momma saucepan, cook all ingredients on low heat until sugar dissolves
- pump up the heat to medium and boil until sugar turns a sexy brown, like Penelope Cruz's hair (about 350°F on a candy thermometer)
- remove from heat, stat, or it will burn and anger you
- add the cream. it will tantrum a bit, then look solid. Don't be concerned
- put back on low heat
- stir incessantly until caramel dissolves
- ***use to your heart's desire***

BARK UP THIS... CHOCOLATE

2 c. chocolate, whatever type you fancy
2 tbsp. fresh ginger, grated
2 tbsp. fresh grated grapefruit zest
1 c. Craisins
1/2 c. slivered almonds
1 tbsp. fresh thyme

- melt chocolate in a double boiler
- add all ingredients, mix
- spread onto a parchment-lined cookie sheet with an edge
- set outside to cool, 'cause you're cool
- break into pieces
- *call yourself a chocoholic with pride*

I'M A WHAT?! KAHLUA TART
WHY YES... YES I AM

1/4 c. unsalted butter
1/2 c. packed brown sugar
2 eggs
2 tbsp. Kahlua
1/2 tsp. lemon juice
1 c. corn syrup
1 batch "Easy as Pie Pastry" *(pg. 47)*

- roll the pastry to fit in cool muffin cups/muffin tins
- the filling goes as follows:
  - create yourself a gooey mess by creaming butter and sugar together
  - beat in everything else
  - pour into pastry shell
- cook at 375°F for approximately 20min.

OPTIONS:

- raisins
- pecans... any nut, really
- chocolate
- sea foam. *I like this*

SPRING
"A FRESH NEW PERSPECTIVE"

EASTER CHICKLETS

Birdy **love** has arrived... soft, round, **fuzzy** newborns call to us to snuggle and enjoy. Resurrecting our senses into a childlike **wonderment** of bunny characters, outdoor chocolate hunts tantalizing our palates with sweet **memories** of all that is **home**.

SPRING HOLLOW

Moving my outdoor pieces inside for a moment **opens** my mind and my french doors to the **gorgeous** new breeze of spring. Preparing my Easter dinner table with **fluffy** babies of all kinds, little gifts of appreciation to my own little chicklets makes me **smile**... spring has arrived!

MENU

Little birdies on a black nest of crunchy twigs... waiting for their eggs to hatch

~ roasted Cornish game hens

~ creamy black lemon vodka pasta

~ fennel seed coleslaw

~ fresh baby quail eggs

Roasted Cornish Game Hens
LITTLE BIRDIES

1 Cornish game hen, per person
handful fresh oregano
2-3 stalks lemongrass
2 garlic cloves
2 tbsp. butter
kosher salt & fresh ground pepper

- stuff hen with oregano, lemon grass and garlic
- coat birdy in butter
- be kind with your salt and pepper
- roast at 400°F for 45min.
- *birdy love has arrived!*

CREAMY BLACK LEMON VODKA PASTA

3 c. whipping cream
1/4 c. lemon vodka
2 shallots & 3 cloves of garlic (minced)
1/2 c. fresh grated parmesan cheese
750g black squid-ink, fresh, or dried pasta
kosher salt & fresh ground pepper

- in a medium saucepan, sautée garlic and shallots until browned
- add remaining ingredients except parmesan cheese and pasta
- bring to a soft rumbling boil and let reduce by half
- while cream sauce is brewing, cook your pasta until el dente and drain
- marry pasta and sauce
- *add cheese, slap your knees, you're a heck of a tease*

Fennel Seed Coleslaw

1 head purple cabbage, chopped
1 head green cabbage, chopped
8 scallions, chopped
1/4 c. sesame seeds
1 fennel, chopped

- mix all ingredients in a bowl
- add dressing *(see below)*

Dressing

1 c. apple cider vinegar
1 c. canola oil
1/2 c. sugar
2 tbsp. fennel seeds
kosher salt & fresh ground pepper

- in a small pot, boil all ingredients until sugar is dissolved

COCO-NUTTY BUNNY CAKES

1/2 c. butter, softened
1 3/4 c. sugar
1 fresh vanilla bean gutt
splash coconut extract
4 egg whites
2 c. flour
1 tsp. baking powder
1/2 tsp. baking soda
1 1/3 c. buttermilk

- cream together butter, sugar, vanilla bean, coconut extract, and egg whites. Set aside
- in a separate bowl, sift together flour, baking powder, and baking soda. Set aside
- in your "purple space", take turns alternating cream mixture, flour mixture, and butter mixture until just combined
- pour into greased silpat cupcake holders or other pretty options
- bake at 350°F 20-22min.

SWEET SOMETHING

1/2 c. butter, softened
1 1/2 tbsp. sweetened condensed milk
splash coconut extract
2 c. icing sugar

- mix it up
- smother your cakes
- *garnish with great ability*

PLAY-FULL

143

KOPETKE
"LITTLE HOOVES"

OMA...

I was ten when I entered sweet **Oma's** kitchen. A God-loving woman with a penchant for always calling me **"sweetheart"**, I fell in love immediately. She sat me down and proceeded to feed me 13 apple **dumplings**. I couldn't eat enough. Between the smell and her loving energy, every bite seemed to **nurture** something deep within me, somewhere beyond my stomach...

Reflecting on that time with Oma, as I **love** and **energize** from my own kitchen, I recognize that the food was one thing, but in my young life it was really her love and kindness that I was most **ravenous** for.

Remembering that now as I prepare meals, I clear my thoughts, my focus being **joy** and **nurturing** so my food doesn't taste grumpy. Whatever happens after that I am usually okay with - **adoration** from all the nibbling souls around me is actually pretty easy to take. As I dedicate this Kopetke recipe to our **OMA**, may you feel every inch of it's delicious ingredients deep in your sweet, **sweet** soul.

KOPETKE

8-10 potatoes
2 eggs
4 c. flour

- boil potatoes until soft, not mushy. Drain, add to stand mixer with 2 eggs
- gradually add flour - be mindful to keep it a soft dough consistency - add sprinkles of h2o if needed
- on a silpat, roll out dough and cut in to "hoove"-like pieces
- in boiling water, add Kopetke until they float to the surface

KOPETKE SAUCE

3 tbsp. butter
splash canola oil
1 white onion, chopped
2 cloves garlic
2 c. mushrooms (any kind is fine)

- heat frying pan to a slight sizzle with butter and canola oil
- add onion, garlic and mushrooms
- saute until golden brown
- with a straining spoon, add Kopetke to frying pan until everything is nicely browned
- set aside
- serve with "provencal herb beef filet" and salad with "creamy balsamic pumpkin seed dressing"

OPTIONS:

- add onion, garlic, or herbs to potato mixture
- stuff with apple, like a dumpling, boiled or sauteed. Serve with sour cream, cinnamon and sugar

PROVENCAL HERB BEEF FILET

4 beef filets
provencal herb (found at local market)
avocado oil
Mirabello balsamic vinegar
kosher salt & fresh ground pepper

- rest on plate, drizzle with oil and venigar (be generous to your liking)
- sprinkle with herbs, salt and pepper. Cover and let sit for a minimum of 4 hr.
- to cook: either BBQ or sear both sides on high heat and finish in oven at 425°F for 15min. depending on thickness of meat. Trust your own discretion

CREAMY BALSAMIC PUMPKINSEED SALAD

1/4 c. mayonaisse
1/4 c. buttermilk
2 sm. garlic cloves, minced
1 tbsp. fresh lemon juice
1 tbsp. Mirabello balsamic vinegar
1/4 c. canola oil
kosher salt & fresh ground black pepper
1 1/2 c. fresh grated parmesan cheese
1-2 c. fresh pumpkin seeds, if available
1 large head of romain lettuce

- in medium-sized bowl, whisk first 9 ingredients together
- bake fresh pumpkin seeds in oven with light oil and salt, until crispy
- wash romain lettuce, then cut or place in large leaves on a pretty plate
- drizzle with dressing, top with pumpkin seeds and add fresh grated parmesan cheese
- *start munching!*

FAMILIA...

All my love is here with me now in the final pages of *Bistro Bene*, these days are about intentional living. I am providing and sustaining the most loving, soft place for my people to land. We enter the shifts of single parenting, adult children coming and going. My mindful meditation is to remain here for them as the juicy center of all they know and hold to be the most important piece of their universe: ~ HOME~

SWEET

ATTACHMENTS

Swagger Chicken

marinate overnight

10-14 drumsticks
2 c. buttermilk
kosher salt & fresh ground pepper
2 c. panko crumbs
1 c. flour
handful fresh thyme (or dill), chopped
3 c. canola oil

- preheat oven to 375°F
- preheat oil in deep pan, for frying
- mix buttermilk, salt and pepper
- soak drumsticks in buttermilk mix, overnight
- on a flat plate, combine panko crumbs, flour, fresh herbs and dash of salt and pepper
- take drumsticks from buttermilk mix, coat in panko crumb mixture
- fry chicken bits until crispy
- transfer to cookie sheet and bake until cooked through
- *find a cool bucket and serve with picnic pizzazz*

JACKER CHICKEN

marinate overnight

10-14 drumsticks
2 c. buttermilk
kosher salt & fresh ground pepper
1 lg. bag Miss Vickie's salt and vinegar chips, crunched to hells and bits

- preheat oven to 375°F
- mix buttermilk, salt and pepper
- soak drumsticks in buttermilk mix, overnight
- on a flat plate, lay out crunched chips
- roll drumsticks in chips, until coated
- bake until fully cooked
- *my idea of "chicken on the way"*

Thyme Jalapeno Corn Bread

handful fresh thyme, chopped
6 jalapenos, chopped
1/2 c. red onion
2 c. aged cheddar, creamy havarti and dutch gouda
3 1/2 c. flour
1 c. corn, removed from cob
1/4 c. sugar
2 tbsp. baking powder
2 c. milk
3 eggs
1 c. butter, melted
1 jar apple jelly

- preheat oven to 350°F
- with your favorite spoon, playfully add flour, sugar and baking powder in a special bowl. Mix about and set aside
- in another little diddy bowl, add all wet ingredients - like goldilocks' porridge, not too lumpy, just lumpy enough
- combine dry and wet together
- mix tasty factors together: thyme, jalapenos, corn, compassion
- grease your pan (loaf or cake)
- bake 30-35min.
- *serve with living gratitude and apple jelly*

TEENY TINY PASTA SALAD

1 bag orzo pasta
handful fresh cilantro or dill
2 sm. scallions, chopped
2 fresh oranges, segmented
zest of one fresh lemon
1/2 c. sundried tomatoes
1/2 c. garlic stuffed olives
3 garlic cloves, chopped
1/4 c. olive oil
1/4 c. apple cider vinegar
1/2 c. crumbled feta
kosher salt & fresh pepper

- cook orzo to bag's instructions
- whisk oil and vinegar together, set aside
- rinse orzo, layer ingredients onto a lovely platter
- add oil and vinegar
- toss and serve
- *go take your neighbour a gift card, smile - you are kind!*

Maple Baby Drumettes

needs marinating

1 c. maple syrup
1/2 c. soy sauce
2 tbsp. chili sauce
1 c. hoison sauce
1 clove fresh garlic
2 tbsp. fresh ginger

- in a small sauce pan mix all ingredients, bring to a light boil
- pour over baby drumettes
- cover and refrigerate overnight (or 2-3hrs.)
- cover with tinfoil bake at 375°F for 40-50min.
- remove tinfoil, bake another 10-15min.
- *serve wearing a pretty ring with fresh chive garnish!*

EARL GREY CHEVRE CHEESECAKE
MAKE EARLY OR RIGHT BEFORE BED

2 bergamont double black earl grey tea bags
* *place tea bags in h2o, set aside, let steep at least 3hr., squeeze extra flavour out when ready to use **
1 log chevre (goat cheese)
4 lg. eggs
3/4 c. sour cream
1 1/3 c. sugar
3 tbsp. warm h2o
2 tbsp. flour

- preheat oven at 350°F
- cream together chevre, sour cream and sugar until light and fluffy-ish
- one at a time, add eggs beating for 30sec. each
- add earl grey tea mix
- add flour
- mix until happy, no over beating please
- put this round, phat pan in a bath
- wrap outside of pan so no water leaks in, place into a roasting pan
- pour water after cheesecake has made itself comfy halfway up the spring form pan (hence the tinfoil)
- bake 70-75min. (no peeking you monkeys) *it will be slightly jiggly in the middle upon finishing...no worries, you just don't want ooey gooey*
- remove pan from h2o
- run a knife around the edge
- let cool, place in fridge to set itself right, uncovered overnight
- *call your mother, tell her you love her and to come for a slice of pure sensory history*

GINGER SNAP CRUST

3 c. crushed ginger snap cookies
1/2 c. butter, melted

- crush snaps with gusto
- mix together
- press into 9" spring form pan

OPTIONS:
- no crust, frozen on a stick, dipped in chocolate
- ginger snap crust

RHUBARB MANGO PORT COULIS

2 c. chopped rhubarb
2 c. chopped mango
1/2 c. port
1/2 c. sugar

- on medium heat, in a heavy bottom saucepan, add all ingredients, cook down until syrupy
- let cool, throw everything into Cuisinart, blend away
- put into pretty jar
- dribble a bit of port on top, take a swig on the side
- *all is good*

HELLO TARYN, YOU'RE A DOLLY

1/4 c. melted butter
1 c. graham cracker crumbs
1 c. chocolate chips
1 c. shredded coconut
1 c. chopped nuts (optional)
1 can sweetened condensed milk

- in a 9"x9" pan pour melted butter and pat in graham crumbs to form a crust
- layer ingredients with the sweetened condensed milk at the top
- bake @ 375°F for 20-25min. or until golden brown
- cut into squares and serve
- *try 'em frozen for crunchy alternative*

I see a hunger here, an observation of **nurture**, perhaps. So, from my heart to my fingertips, I create meals and a home designed on the true intention that if all is well on an emotional level under the roof of my life…

…then not only do I heal my own story, but my children get to enjoy a present mumma who reminds us - no matter what - there is always beauty in a world where there is *love, ambiance, and food.*

SERENDIPITOUS

RECIPE INDEX

SUMMER...

All up in Your Grill... Boat? - 46
Applewood Grill - 41
Aussie Salad, The - 30
Balsamic Onions - 53
Balsamic Reduction - 45
Basil Brie Grill - 40
Beef Filet - 23
Beef Sliders - 24
Beergarita - 18
Beets - 30
Bloomin' Plum Turnovers - 39
Blueberry Compote - 27
Buffalo Mozza Grill - 42
Boozy Frosty Bits - 56
Boozy Strawberry Choco"Latte" Cake - 55
Borscht - 17
Buttermilk Cake - 27
Caramelized Bacon - 56
Chocolate Covered Chips - 52
Cotton Cloud Glaze - 54
Counter Staple Lemon Loaf - 37
Cozy Pig Tubes - 53
Crunchy Rice - 31
Easy as Pie Pastry - 47

Food Swag - 52
Garlic Fennel Butter - 46
Grainy Mashed Potatoes - 17
Grilly Cheeses for the AM that will Blow your Mind - 40
I'm Sweet, He's Sour, Chicken - 33
Mango Mayonnaise - 32
Maple Dressing - 30
"O Honey Dew, Meet Your Fennel Friend" Salad - 21
"Once Upon a Time there was a Mango, She was Lonely for Beef..." - 23
Pick 'em and Grab 'em Platter - 50
Poison Ribs - 31
Prawns, 10 or So - 24
Raspberry Lemongrass Pie - 47
"Red Deer" Sauce - 24
Smashed Tatoes - 31
Stabbed Strawberries with Balsamic Reduction - 45
Strawberry Balsamic Jam (I Love The Middle) - 56
Strawberry Rhubarb Peppercorn Jam - 37
Sweet Sour Sauce - 33
Sweet Taters - 53
Tomato Orange Compote - 32
Vanilla Bean Cotton Cloud Cake - 54
Warmed Potato Salad - 20

Wasabi Mayo - 24
Watermelon Basil Salad - 21
When Lamb Hangs with Beef... this Happens Burgers - 32
Whipped Cream (I Love the Middle) - 56
Whipped Cream Topping - 27
"You're Such an Aioli" Sauce - 53

AUTUMN...

Autumn Soup - 82
Baked Pumpkin Slice with Coffee Yogurt - 100
Basil Buffalo Mozzaaa - 106
B.B.B.S. - 87
Beef Tenderloin Roast - 93
Boy Beefy Dip - 94
Breakfast Dough Nuggets - 97
Brothy Balsamic Reduction - 95
Caramelized Onion Zzaaa - 105
C.C.C. Sauce - 70
"Cheeky Cheesy Chicky" Poutine - 70
Chocolate Pumpkin Pie - 89
Crepes - 75
Crispy Fry Wedges - 71
Crusty Top - 95

RECIPE INDEX

...AUTUMN

Dippity Doo - 94
Don't be a Turkey... Dinner - 83
Drops of Choco-Cocoa-Nut - 76
Freaking Fantastic Stuffing - 85
French Kissed Onion Soup - 92
Fresh Figgy Cranberry Compote - 88
Giblet Gravy - 84
Horsey Mayo - 93
I Like your Rack...of Lamb - 95
'm Almost as Wild as this... Mushroom Soup - 81
Karamel Apple Babies - 63
Maple Infused Yams - 86
Maple Marnier Bouillie with Brown Sugar - 98
Mmm Roasted Apples - 80
Oh Hello! Taco in a Bag - 72
Pop... and it's Over - 75
Pork me Jack (Apples) - 96
Protein Balls - 76
Roasted Sunday Chicken - 69
Saucy Sauce - 95
Smoked Oyster & Quail Egg Benedict - 99
Whipped Potatoes - 86

Whipped Cream - 89
Warmed Chocolate Love in a Cup - 60
Stewed Tomato White Bean Compote - 99
Stuffed Dough - 101
Stuffed Pizza - 103
Thin Crust Dough - 102
Tomato Sauce - 101

WINTER...

Bark up This... Chocolate - 127
Cranberry White Chocolate Biscotti - 115
Ginger, What Kinda Cake Did You Say? - 124
I'm a what?! Kahlua Tart - 128
Lovely Layers Like You've Never Seen Before - 122
Sexy Caramel - 126
Sparkly Snowflake Sweeties - 117
Sticky Nikki's Gooey Mess - 123

SPRING...

Coco-Nutty Bunny Cakes - 142

Creamy Balsamic Pumpkin Seed Salad - 148
Creamy Black Lemon Vodka Pasta - 138
Earl Grey Chevre Cheesecake - 158
Fennel Seed Coleslaw & Dressing - 139
Ginger Snap Crust - 158
Hello Taryn, You're a Dolly - 160
Jacker Chicken - 154
Kopetke - 148
Maple Baby Drumettes - 157
Provencal Herb Beef Filet - 148
Rhubarb Mango Port Coulis - 159
Roasted Cornish Game Hens - 136
Swagger Chicken - 153
Sweet Something - 142
Teeny Tiny Pasta Salad - 156
Thyme Jalapeno Cornbread - 155

-Love Chef Elle

To the Team:
Taryn Adrian & Trevor DeGraff

The creation of this lovely book would not exist without the brilliance of your complimentary skillsets. I'll never forget the photoshoots, food testing, and the endless hours of editing.

You believed in me when I was a new chef, divorcée, and really had no business making a cookbook. But, I'm a bad ass and did it anyway, and so are the both of you.

Endless gratitude...

– Chef Elle

www.ingramcontent.com/pod-product-compliance
Lightning Source LLC
Chambersburg PA
CBRC101245160426
43209CB00025B/1893